DK eyewonder

Bugs

Penguin Random House

LONDON, NEW YORK,
MELBOURNE, MUNICH, and DELHI

Written and edited by Penelope York
US editors Gary Werner and Margaret Parrish
Designed by Janet Allis
Managing editor Sue Leonard
Managing art editor Rachael Foster
Picture researcher Jo Haddon
Production Kate Oliver
Jacket designer Chris Drew
DTP designer Almudena Diaz
Consultant Paul Pearce-Kelly

REVISED EDITION
DK UK

Senior editor Caroline Stamps
Senior art editor Rachael Grady
US editor Margaret Parrish
Jacket editor Manisha Majithia
Jacket designer Natasha Rees
Jacket design development manager
Sophia M Tampakopoulos Turner
Producer (print production) Mary Slater
Producer (pre-production) Rachel Ng
Publisher Andrew Macintyre

DK INDIA

Senior editor Shatarupa Chaudhuri
Senior art editor Rajnish Kashyap
Assistant editor Suneha Dutta
Assistant art editor Vidit Vashisht
Managing editor Alka Thakur Hazarika
Managing art editor Romi Chakraborty
DTP designer Dheeraj Singh
Picture researcher Sumedha Chopra

First American Edition, 2002
This American Edition, 2015
Published in the United States by DK Publishing
4th floor, 345 Hudson Street
New York, New York 10014
14 15 16 17 18 10 9 8 7 6 5 4 3 2 1
001—196637—02/2015

A catalog record for this book is available
from the Library of Congress.
ISBN 978-1-4654-1854-8

DK books are available at special discounts when purchased in
bulk for sales promotions, premiums, fund-raising, or educational
use. For details, contact: DK Publishing Special Markets,
4th floor, 345 Hudson Street, New York, New York 10014 or
SpecialSales@dk.com.

Color reproduction by Scanhouse, Malaysia
Printed and bound in China by Hung Hing

Discover more at
www.dk.com

Contents

Bugs, bugs, bugs

Most of the bugs that you know are called arthropods, which means that their skeletons are on the outside of their bodies. There are more than a million known species of arthropod on the Earth. Here are a few types to look for.

Trapped in time

We know that insects were around over 40 million years ago because some were trapped in a substance called amber, which then hardened.

Thorax

Head

Abdomen

What is an insect?

You can spot an insect by counting its body parts and legs. All insects have six legs and three body parts—a head, a thorax, and an abdomen.

What is a myriapod?

If you try counting the legs on a creepy crawly and find you can't, chances are you are looking at a myriapod, such as a millipede or centipede. They have many segments and lots and lots of legs!

Extreme bugs

● The petroleum fly lives in puddles of crude oil and feeds on insects that get stuck in it.

● Some midges can be put into boiling water and survive.

● Snow fleas can survive in subzero temperatures. If you pick one up, it will die in the heat of your hand.

What is an arachnid?

All arachnids have eight legs. Watch out, however: other than spiders, a lot of arachnids look like insects, so count carefully.

What is a true bug?

These days we tend to call all creepy crawlies "bugs"—as we have in this book. But, in fact, a true bug is a type of insect that has a long mouthpart. The bug uses it to pierce food and then suck up the inside of the food.

Leapers and creepers

Some bugs are speedy, some are slow. Some bugs run and others jump. They all have their reasons for doing what they do, and a lot depends on where they live—different obstacles demand different types of movement.

High jump
The flea is the most powerful jumper of all insects. It has a little spring in its legs to enable it to jump very high. It can jump 600 times an hour for three days when it is looking for a host.

Speed demon
The green tiger beetle is the fastest insect on land. It runs at 3½ ft (1 m) per second. It uses its speed to catch other insects and to run quickly across the hot desert sand.

Leaps and bounds
If a grasshopper or cricket is disturbed and it needs to get away, it uses its massively developed, muscle-packed legs to leap high into the air.

A grasshopper can leap 20 times the length of its body.

Looping upward
Some caterpillars loop their way up branches. They attach their back leg suckers to the branch and stretch their bodies forward, then loop up their backs, pulling the suckers upward. They can walk up some pretty steep twigs.

Keeping in step
A millipede has up to 180 pairs of legs! They all help it force its way through the soil. It has to be very coordinated when it walks, otherwise its legs would bump into each other. It moves them in waves.

Up, up, and away

Creepy crawlies are the ultimate explorers—
they can get anywhere and everywhere. This is
because many of them have wings. Flying insects
have two pairs of wings, but use them in different
ways. All, however, are experts in aerobatics.

Liftoff
The lacewing flutters
gracefully using all four
wings. It can control
each pair separately,
allowing it to turn
easily and even
fly backward.

Flutter by
The butterfly flaps all its
wings at the same time
at about five beats per
second. Its wings are
delicate and it has to be
careful that it doesn't
damage them.

Gone in a flash!
The little hoverfly can beat
its wings up to 1,000 times per
second. Sometimes it flies too
quickly to be seen. It hovers
in the air, then darts away so
quickly that it seems to disappear.

Cruise control

The second set of wings on the crane fly has turned into halteres that look like drumsticks. The crane fly uses these for balance and coordination, and to change direction in a split second.

Haltere

A hard case

The beetle only uses one pair of wings to fly. Its front wings have become hard cases that protect the flying wings when they are folded away.

THE INCREDIBLE JOURNEY

When the winter cold arrives in the Rocky Mountains, the monarch butterfly migrates up to 3,000 miles (4,828 km) to the warmer weather in California and Mexico. It covers 80 miles (129 km) a day and travels in huge groups. At the end of their journey, the groups always settle on the same tree as the year before. No one knows how they find their way.

Making sense

Imagine being able to taste with your feet, or having eyes as big as your head. Sound odd? Well, bugs have some pretty strange ways to find their way around and sniff each other out.

Feeling the way

Some insects, such as this cave cricket, live in dark places where there is little light. Because of this, their eyesight is not good. Instead, they use long feelers, or "antennae," which stop them from bumping into walls all the time in the pitch dark.

Powerful perfume

Antennae are also used to smell. This male moth has two hairy antennae that can smell a female moth from 6½ miles (11 km) away!

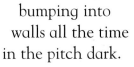

A matter of taste

This butterfly tastes with its feet. When it lands on a particularly tasty flower, its long mouthparts, or "proboscis," unfold automatically and allow it to drink.

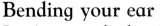

Bending your ear

Bugs' ears can be found on their wings, bellies, or heads and, believe it or not, this katydid listens with its knees! The slits on the legs are ears that can pick up other crickets' calls.

Bug-eyed
The horsefly's enormous eyes take up almost all of its head. Its eyes are very sensitive to movement, which is why it is so incredibly difficult to swat.

Meat-eaters

There are so many bugs around, you would think it would be easy for predators to catch and eat them. Think again! Hunters have to invent cunning ways to get their dinner, and they have weird ways to eat it, too.

The waiting game
A praying mantis hides camouflaged among leaves, where it sits still for a very long time, with its forelegs ready to strike. When an insect passes, it pounces at lightning speed and chews it up in its jaws.

Wrap it up

The spider waits patiently in its web for an insect to fly into it. It then wraps the bug up in a jacket of silk to stop it from moving, injects it with venom, and then sucks out its insides.

Dragonflies need a lot of wing skills to catch a bug in flight.

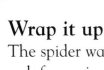

It takes the orb web spider about an hour to spin a web.

Fast food

Hawker dragonflies are so nimble and speedy that they can catch insects in midair. They grab a passing insect with their powerful jaws and grip it with their long legs.

Little suckers

The assassin bug is a typical piercer and sucker. After catching its prey, it pierces the body, injecting saliva to turn the inside of the prey into liquid. Then the assassin sucks it dry.

The trapdoor spider spends most of its life waiting for its next meal.

Knock, knock!

The trapdoor spider makes a hole for itself underground and weaves a trapdoor of dirt and silk. When an unsuspecting insect wanders over the door, the spider is out like a shot to snatch it and gobble it up.

Cunning carnivores

● The Portia spider from Australia taps on the webs of other spiders, pretending to be a fly. When the spider arrives to eat the fly, the Portia eats it!

● The ant lion larva buries itself in the ground with its mouth facing the sky. When an ant runs over it, it falls right into its jaws and is swiftly eaten.

Bug veggies

Many bugs in the world are vegetarians and munch like crazy during their short lives. Some pierce, then suck up their food, and others bite and chew it; but, however they eat, they eat a lot.

Army of eaters

Caterpillars have huge appetites. They are biters and chewers and have to nibble constantly to grow into adults. They have powerful jaws and strong teeth that enable them to chew through tough leaves.

Liquid lunch

When the caterpillar grows into a butterfly, it changes its eating habits. It feeds on liquids, which it sucks up using its long, hollow tongue (the proboscis) like a straw.

Heavy-duty chewing

You wouldn't eat wood, but this stag beetle larva loves it. It eats and eats rotten wood until it is fat enough to turn into a beetle.

When butterflies and moths are not hungry, they roll their tongues into tight, curly coils.

14

Nuts about nuts

The acorn weevil feeds only on acorns. It pierces the hard nut with its long snout and chomps away with the strong jaws it has at the end of its snout. It then sucks the food up the snout into its body.

This weevil also lays its eggs in acorns.

Now you see me...

Lurking in the undergrowth, there are many bugs that look like bugs and many that don't. Cunning camouflages help some bugs to catch a meal and others to keep from becoming one.

Flower power

If you look carefully at these beautiful flowers, you will be able to see the shape of an orchid mantis. It can change color from white to pink to blend in with the particular flower it is sitting on.

Spiked survivors

Birds are not going to risk landing on a prickly branch, so what better disguise than to look like a spiked thorn—as long as these treehopper bugs keep still.

Lost among leaves

As long as this leaf-mimic katydid sticks to the right leaves, it definitely won't be spotted. It even has veins on its back just like the real leaves.

Dropping in

Yuck! That bird dropping doesn't look very good to eat. Wrong—it's actually a very tasty king swallowtail butterfly caterpillar.

Twiggy

At first glance, what you see is just a boring twig. Look again. This walking stick insect's disguise helps protect it from predators.

MOTH STORY

Once upon a time in England, there lived pale-colored peppered moths that hid on light-colored tree bark. By the late 19th century, the moths mysteriously started to become darker. Eventually, it became clear that the moths were darker because pollution from factories had darkened the trees. Only the darker moths remained camouflaged, and they were the only ones that survived.

Playing dead

Look closely at these dead leaves—one of them is very much alive. The cryptic moth sits on the decaying leaf and is almost invisible. No one is going to spot it.

Warning signals

Some bugs make it obvious to their attackers that they would be nasty to eat. They make "Don't eat me or you'll be sorry" known in various ways. Others have methods that startle hunters, and a few use clever disguises.

Snake scare

It may look like a snake, but it's actually a caterpillar! This crafty creature is safe from hunters. Who would risk eating a snake?

Making eyes

Imagine taking a quick glance at this little banana eater butterfly. You'd think that those eyes were on a much bigger and more ferocious beast.

Hot bomb

A bombardier beetle under attack has a deadly revenge. It squirts a chemical out of its backside at high speed and at a temperature of nearly 212°F (100°C)!

Ultimate defense

When attacked, the puss moth caterpillar rears up its colorful head. Bright colors warn predators that a bug is poisonous, so they leave it alone.

Weta whack

Disturb the enormous weta cricket and you are in for a shock. Quick as a flash, it shoots its back legs up to deliver a sharp kick.

Copycat

Some bugs are lazy. They are not poisonous, so they copy the colors of something that is, and they are left alone. Can you tell the difference between the bee with a sting and the harmless hoverfly? No? Good disguise! The bee is on the left.

Mother care

Most creepy crawlies lay eggs and abandon them to fend for themselves. Others make sure that the eggs will hatch on their first meal, and a few take very good care of their young.

Doomed!

The parasitic wasp lays its eggs on a live caterpillar, which can't shake them off. The caterpillar continues to get fatter and juicier until the eggs hatch and gobble it up. It makes a yummy first meal!

Born alive

The aphid is a weird breeder. It gives birth to live young—unusual for an insect—and doesn't need to mate to give birth. If every aphid survived, each one would produce billions more within six months. Luckily for us, lots of bugs eat aphids, otherwise we would be overrun!

Protective shield

The mother shieldbug looks after her young with great care. Sometimes she glues her eggs to the male's back, and he cares for them until they hatch! When they are born, she guards them fiercely.

An aphid being born

Piggyback ride

The jungle scorpion is a very good mom. She gives birth to live young, catching them as they are born. She puts them onto her back for two weeks until they are strong enough to fend for themselves. She can carry up to 30 babies at a time.

21

All change

Some insects start their lives looking completely different from their adult shape. When they are ready, certain insects, such as caterpillars, undergo a sudden change and emerge with a new image. Others change slowly and steadily.

1 Caterpillar stage

The blue morpho butterfly starts off as a small, hairy caterpillar that eats and eats and eats, until...

2 Pupa stage

... it sheds its skin and creates a pupa. A transformation happens inside, and one day...

3 Emerging

... the pupa splits and a completely new-looking insect starts to emerge. It pushes itself out until...

4 Butterfly

... it stretches out its crumpled wings and flies away as a beautiful butterfly. The change is called metamorphosis, and it happens to many creatures in the insect world.

Shedding skin

Some insects change slowly as they grow, such as this dragonfly. Because an insect's skeleton, which is on the outside of its body, does not grow, it has to replace its skin to grow bigger. This dragonfly is shedding its skin for the last time.

23

Buzzing around

If you hear a buzzing sound in your yard, chances are you are listening to something that stings, such as a bee or a wasp. But there is more to these buzzing bugs than meets the eye. They build some incredible homes and are excellent team players.

Collecting nectar

During the spring and summer, honeybees fly from flower to flower to gather nectar. Back in the hive, the bees use the nectar to make honey.

A hive of activity

Honeybees live in hives. Inside the hive they make a honeycomb, which is made out of wax from their glands. The six-sided cells that make up the honeycomb hold honey and eggs, which the queen bee lays.

Bee dance

When a worker bee finds a good nectar supply, it returns home to the hive and does a little "figure-eight" dance, which lets the other bees know where the nectar is.

Building a nest

Some wasps live in large nests made of paper. The queen wasp starts the nest by chewing dead wood, mixing it with saliva and letting it dry. She then lays eggs, which hatch, and the next generation continues with the nest-building.

Sweet tooth

Wasps love sugar and especially sweet fruits, which is why they buzz around your food in the summer, annoying you. They won't sting you, however, unless you threaten them.

Army of helpers

Ants and termites live in huge
colonies where they build
their homes together, work
together, and never have
time for play. Their entire
lives revolve around bringing
up their young safely.

Loyal subjects

The queen termite is
a huge, ugly, egg-laying
machine that never moves
from her royal chamber.
The termites rally around
her, feeding and
cleaning her.

Termite high-rise

Some species of termite
live in huge mounds
that they build using dirt,
saliva, and their droppings.
The mounds can be up
to 20 ft (6 m) high.

*The king termite lives with
the queen in her nest.*

Big bully

The toughest ant around is the Australian bulldog ant. It grips its meal in its huge, powerful jaws, then swings its body around and stings the prey from behind. Bugs that get in its way don't stand a chance!

Fast friends

Ants and aphids are very good at keeping each other happy. The aphids eat a lot of tree sap and give off a sweet liquid that the ants like to sip. In return, the ants guard the aphids from predators.

Lots of bugs like to eat aphids, so having ant bodyguards is the best way for aphids to survive.

THE ANT CLEANING SERVICE

Every so often, villagers in Africa receive a visit from a march of up to 22 million driver ants that forces them out of their homes. Although each ant is only ⅜ in (1 cm) long and blind, the swarm kills every pest that gets in its way, such as locusts and scorpions. The villagers welcome the clean-up crew!

Teamwork

Some ants build their nests by weaving together groups of leaves. They each carry a live ant larva in their jaws and make it produce silk, which they then use to sew up the leaves. If anyone threatens the nest, they attack by biting.

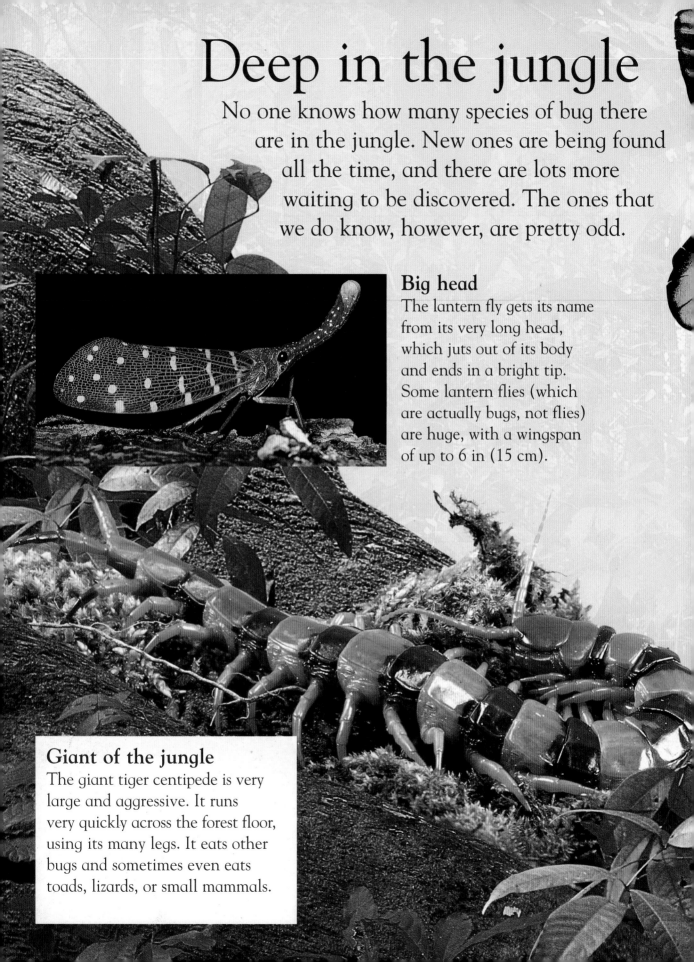

Deep in the jungle

No one knows how many species of bug there are in the jungle. New ones are being found all the time, and there are lots more waiting to be discovered. The ones that we do know, however, are pretty odd.

Big head

The lantern fly gets its name from its very long head, which juts out of its body and ends in a bright tip. Some lantern flies (which are actually bugs, not flies) are huge, with a wingspan of up to 6 in (15 cm).

Giant of the jungle

The giant tiger centipede is very large and aggressive. It runs very quickly across the forest floor, using its many legs. It eats other bugs and sometimes even eats toads, lizards, or small mammals.

Queen of flight

The Queen Alexandra's birdwing is the largest butterfly in the world, and one of the rarest. Its wingspan can reach 11 in (28 cm).

Tiny and spiny

The postman butterfly caterpillar has sharp spikes all over its soft body. These spikes protect it from predators. It feeds on poisonous passion flower leaves that are absorbed into its body and make it poisonous, too.

Hairy, scary spider

During the day, the red-kneed tarantula sleeps in its silk-lined burrow. When the Sun goes down, the tarantula emerges for the night hunt, searching for large insects and injecting them with venom.

Sand devils

The desert is a tough place to live. Not many plants grow there, and there is little water around. Bugs need to be pretty sharp if they are going to survive in one of the hottest places on Earth.

Honeypot pantry

The honeypot ant workers feed other honeypot ants with lots of nectar, which they store in their huge tummies. When food is scarce, the ants with the potbellies vomit up the honey that they have made and feed it to the workers.

Jewel of the desert

The jewel wasp is solitary—it lives alone. Here, it stings a cockroach, before laying its eggs on the roach. The roach will be the first meal for the youngsters.

The store ants spend all their lives hanging from the ceiling.

Best pals
Without each other, the yucca moth and the yucca plant wouldn't survive. The moth lays its eggs on the plant and in return pollinates it as it does so. The newborn caterpillars eat the seeds, but leave enough for new plants to grow.

Dew drinker
The darkling beetle has a slick way of finding the water it needs. It waits until morning, when dew has formed on its back, then leans forward and catches the dew as it trickles into its mouth.

A sting in the tail
This desert scorpion hardly ever needs to drink. It gets most of its moisture from the spiders and insects that it eats. Its sting is so poisonous that it could kill a person.

Desert carpet
Large swarms of these desert locusts eat in the cool of the night and rest during the day's heat. Sometimes, there are so many that they look like a huge desert carpet.

Water world

If you find a body of water, chances are it is filled with mini life—but you may have to look closely to see some of it. Many bugs live in, or above, the water, and some can even walk on the surface.

Diving in

The diving beetle is the great meat-eater of the water. It tucks a bubble of air under its wings so it can breathe underwater, and dives down to catch tadpoles and even small fish.

Walking on water

Pond skaters can walk on water because of thick, waterproof hairs on their feet. They skim over the surface looking for floating food.

Darting around

The beautiful dragonfly lives above water. It is called the dragonfly because of its very aggressive "dragon-like" behavior.

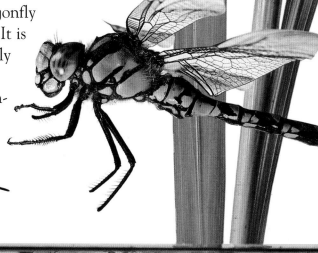

Bottoms up!

Mosquito larvae live in the water. When they need air, they swim to the surface and hang there with their snorkel-like breathing tubes poking up through the top.

Back stroke

The water boatman hangs upside down just beneath the surface. It looks like a little boat, and its back legs are just like oars, which is how it got its name.

Caddis armor

The larva of the caddis fly builds a case around itself to protect it. It makes the case out of stones, shells, and pieces of plants.

Watery web

The air-breathing water spider makes a diving bell in which to live. It makes a web underwater, among the plants, and stocks it with air from the surface.

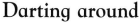

Little mites

This house dust mite is 0.001 in (0.3 mm) long and eats flakes of your dead skin. You have millions of dust mites in your home, which live in mattresses, furniture, and carpets. They can cause people to sneeze and wheeze.

House mites

You may try to forget that bugs live all over your home, but the fact is they are there. They may not all be nasty, but they have one thing in common—they like living with us.

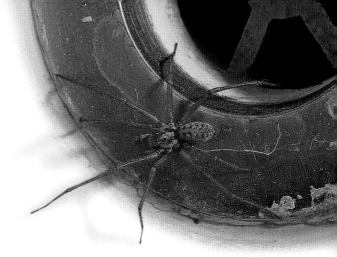

Spiders in the home
The house spider likes to live in dark places in your home, such as down the drain. Sometimes you will spot it scuttling across the floor to eat flies and other bugs.

What a louse!
Once a female head louse has a tight grip on one of your hairs, she is very difficult to get rid of. She can lay 50 eggs (nits), each at the base of a single hair. She causes your head to itch because she sucks blood from your scalp.

Fly alert!
Flies love to share the food you eat. They vomit their digestive juices onto your meal, turning it into liquid that they suck up into their bodies.

Unwanted guests
Cockroaches are badly behaved visitors. They eat anything tasty they can find in the home and, once settled, are very difficult to get rid of.

As dusk falls...

As day turns into night, some insects are just starting to wake up. Whether they are trying to keep from being eaten, or getting ready to have a meal, nighttime is a pretty lively time in bug land.

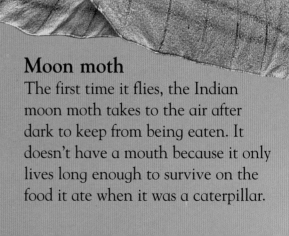

Moon moth
The first time it flies, the Indian moon moth takes to the air after dark to keep from being eaten. It doesn't have a mouth because it only lives long enough to survive on the food it ate when it was a caterpillar.

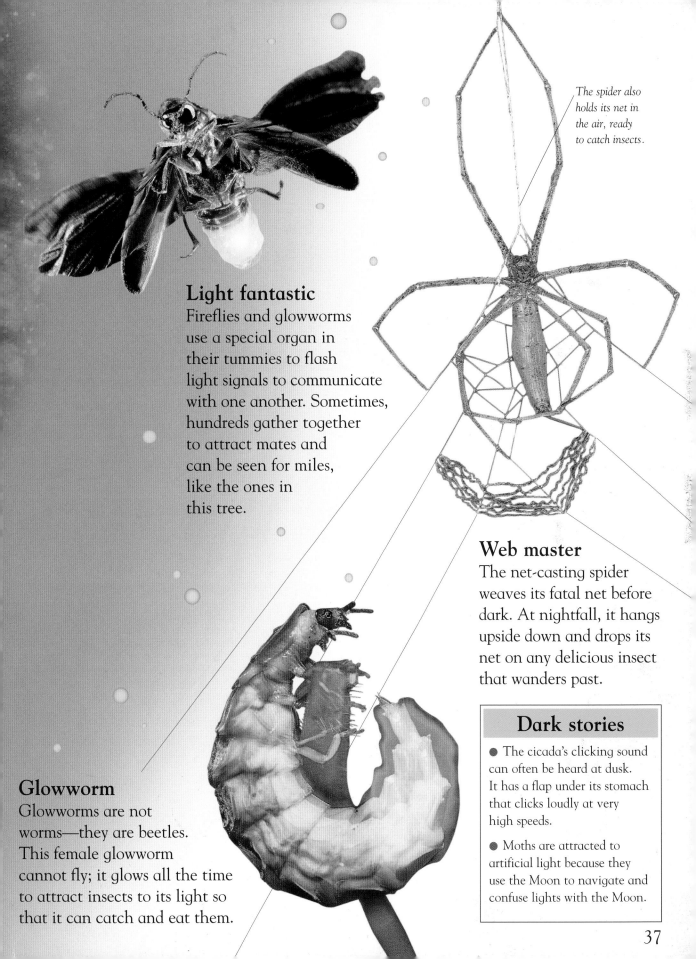

The spider also holds its net in the air, ready to catch insects.

Light fantastic

Fireflies and glowworms use a special organ in their tummies to flash light signals to communicate with one another. Sometimes, hundreds gather together to attract mates and can be seen for miles, like the ones in this tree.

Web master

The net-casting spider weaves its fatal net before dark. At nightfall, it hangs upside down and drops its net on any delicious insect that wanders past.

Dark stories

● The cicada's clicking sound can often be heard at dusk. It has a flap under its stomach that clicks loudly at very high speeds.

● Moths are attracted to artificial light because they use the Moon to navigate and confuse lights with the Moon.

Glowworm

Glowworms are not worms—they are beetles. This female glowworm cannot fly; it glows all the time to attract insects to its light so that it can catch and eat them.

Weird and wonderful

So many bugs have evolved mysterious habits and strange looks that they could fill a whole book. Here is a small selection from around the world.

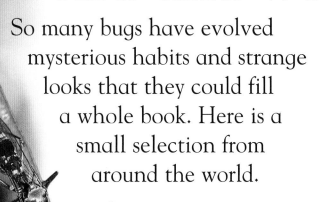

How weird would it be to have eyes on the end of stalks?

Terrifying taste

The flambeau butterfly has very strange taste in food. It sits on an alligator's eyes and sips its tears. What a brave little bug!

Eyes on stalks

The eyes of stalk-eyed flies are on the top of long stalks. When two males meet they compare eyes, and the one with the widest set gets the girl.

Stick your neck out

Why does the giraffe weevil have such a long neck? No one knows. But it certainly makes it one of the weirdest-looking bugs.

Mystical mantis

You can barely tell which way around this mantis nymph is facing. If you look carefully, however, you can just see its head on the right-hand side. Its strange coloring helps it to camouflage itself.

Out of this world

If you came across this katydid in the jungle, with its spiny body and strange colors, you'd be forgiven for thinking that the Earth had just been invaded by aliens!

Pests and plagues

They may be small, but bugs can do a surprising amount of damage, in large numbers or on their own. We humans sometimes have to try hard to control them, and very often we lose.

Leaping locusts

Imagine a swarm of a billion locusts. Yuck! A swarm this big, which we call a plague, can eat every crop in a region in a matter of hours. When there are so many locusts together at once, they blot out the Sun as they pass overhead.

Colorado killer

In 1850, settlers arrived in the Rocky Mountains and they brought with them the potato. These tiny Colorado beetles got a taste for potatoes and swept across the US, eating the whole crop. They are still a serious pest.

Deadly skeeter

The deadly mosquito is the world's most dangerous animal. It can spread a disease called malaria when it sucks blood, and it has been responsible for killing more humans than any other living creature.

Only female mosquitos drink blood.

It's all in the kiss

The kissing bug likes to suck blood from near a human's mouth. It leaves its droppings near the bite, which can get scratched into the skin, resulting in an illness called Chagas disease.

Big sucker

This tsetse fly is filled with blood that it has just sucked out of a human. But not only does it leave an itch, but it can also leave behind a deadly disease called sleeping sickness.

A DEADLY TALE

In the past, when someone old was dying, their relatives sat up with them all night to watch them. Often the sitters would hear an eerie tap, tap, tap coming from the wooden walls. It was a small beetle that eats through wood. When it hatches from its egg, it bangs its head against the wood to attract another beetle to it, making a tapping sound. That's how it got its name—the death-watch beetle.

Cleaning up

Nature has its own recycling service in the form of bugs that feed on dead plants, animals, and dung. Left uneaten, the remains would build up into a huge pile of rotten gunge. We should be very thankful for these small cleaners!

Feeding frenzy

Maggots are specialists when it comes to eating decaying flesh. Flies lay their eggs on rotting animals. The eggs hatch into maggots. The maggots' streamlined shape helps them burrow into the flesh to eat it.

Great balls of dung

When a pile of dung appears in Africa, the dung beetles rush in, each one claiming a piece of the action. The male makes a perfect ball of dung, rolls it away, and buries it. The female lays a single egg in the ball. When the egg hatches, the beetle grub (larva) eats the dung.

Cleaning agents

Millipedes live in damp, dark areas
and are very useful cleaners. They
eat any rotting leaves and dead bugs
lying around, breaking them down
to become part of the soil again.

DUNG DISPOSAL

When Europeans arrived in Australia, they brought
cows with them (there were none there already).
The dung beetles in Australia were used to dry
kangaroo pellets, not the soft cowpats, and
the pile of cowpats got larger and the flies got
worse until an answer had to be found. So the
Europeans introduced African dung beetles—
which were used to soft dung—to Australia.
The Australians now enjoy a fast rate of disposal.

The essential bug

Whether you like them or not, bugs are an essential part of our lives. We spend a lot of time trying to get rid of them, but we could not live without them.

Cricket crunch

About 500 types of insect provide a good, healthy snack for people around the world. These crickets add a nice crunch to these lollipops.

Honey bee

Bees help plants pollinate by moving pollen from flower to flower. Without them, we wouldn't have nearly as many plants as we do. Bees also supply us with lots of sweet honey.

Silky threads

Did you know that when you wear silk you are actually wearing material made by a caterpillar? When the silk moth caterpillar pupates, it makes a silk lining for its cocoon, which we use to weave into cloth.

Useful facts

● The African leaf beetle is so poisonous that South African bushmen put the poison onto their arrows to kill their prey.

● Red food coloring (cochineal) is taken from the crushed bodies of scale insects.

● Some insects are used in medicine. Bee venom is said to help people with bad joints.

Pest control

Sometimes insects, such as these aphids, multiply so quickly that they eat huge amounts of our crops. The best way to get rid of them, without poisoning, is to introduce other insects that eat them, such as the ladybug.

This is known as biological pest control.

True or false?

Enter the world of bugs and see if you can find what is true and what is false in this mini quiz.

All arachnids have **eight legs**.
See page 4

Flying insects have four pairs of wings.
See page 8

The **jungle scorpion** can carry up to 100 babies at a time on its back.
See page 21

The flambeau butterfly drinks the **tears of a lion**.
See page 38

The **giant tiger centipede** can eat toads and small mammals.
See page 28

Pond skaters look for food underwater.
See page 33

A swarm of millions of locusts is called a **plague**.
See page 40

An insect has six legs and four body parts.
See page 4

Butterflies use their long, hollow tongues like straws **to feed**.
See page 14

The **acorn weevil** not only eats acorns, but also lays its eggs in them.
See page 15

The lantern fly is actually a bug, **not a fly**.
See page 28

Honey trail

The honeybee is trying to go back home after collecting nectar. Answer the questions correctly to lead it to its hive.

Honeycomb is made of...
See page 24

plastic

wax

laugh

START

When bees find a good nectar supply, they...
See page 24

sing

silk

dance

leaves

Nectar is collected from...
See page 24

trees

flowers

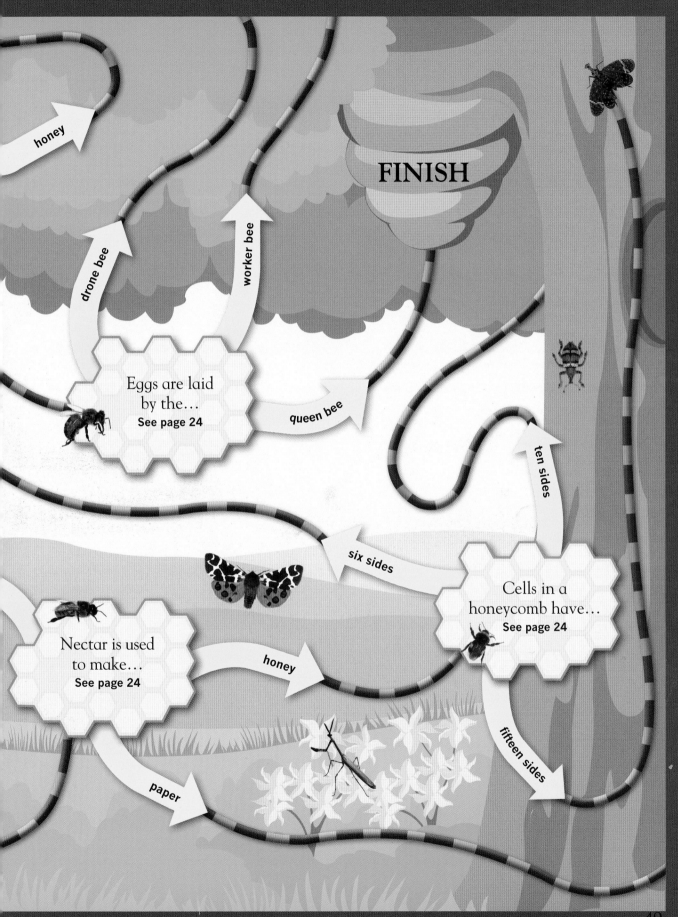

honey

drone bee

worker bee

FINISH

Eggs are laid
by the…
See page 24

queen bee

ten sides

six sides

Cells in a
honeycomb have…
See page 24

Nectar is used
to make…
See page 24

honey

paper

fifteen sides

Facts matchup

How much do you know about the bugs of the world? Read the clues below and see if you can find the correct answers among the pictures.

Desert scorpion

Tsetse fly

Red-kneed tarantula

Treehopper bug

Shieldbug

Orchid mantis

The slits on my knees are ears that can pick up crickets' calls. **See page 10**

Using my muscle-packed legs, I can leap 20 times the length of my body. **See page 7**

I don't have a mouth because I only live long enough to survive on the food I ate when I was a caterpillar. **See page 36**

My front wings have become hard cases that protect my flying wings when they are folded away. **See page 9**

I can catch insects in midair by grabbing them with my powerful jaws and gripping them with my long legs. **See page 13**

I hardly need to drink. I get most of my moisture from the spiders and insects I eat. **See page 31**

Once I catch my prey, I pierce its body and inject saliva to turn the inside of the prey into liquid. **See page 13**

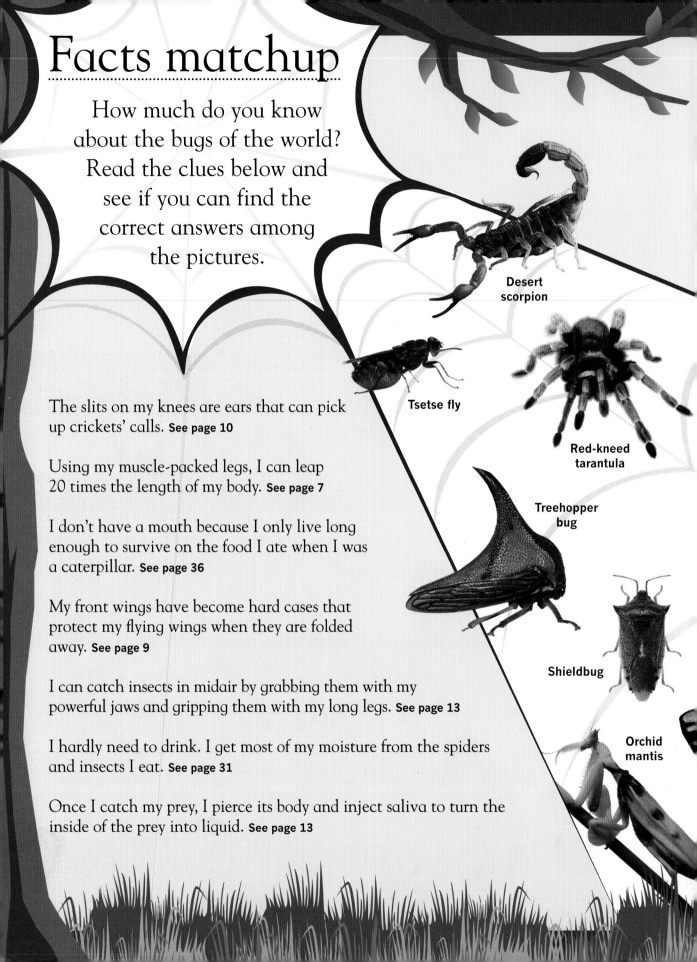

I sometimes glue my eggs to the male's back, and he looks after them until they hatch. **See page 21**

I disguise myself to look like a spiked thorn on a branch so that birds don't risk landing on me. **See page 16**

When an insect wanders over my underground hole, I snatch it and eat it. **See page 13**

I can change color from white to pink to blend in with the particular flower I choose to sit on. **See page 16**

My brightly colored head warns predators that I'm poisonous and should be left alone. **See page 18**

During the day, I sleep in my silk-lined burrow. When it gets dark, I go out to hunt for large insects. **See page 29**

I do a "figure-eight" dance when I find a nectar supply. This lets the others know where the nectar is. **See page 24**

My bite not only leaves an itch, but can also cause a deadly disease called sleeping sickness. **See page 41**

I am the largest butterfly in the world, and one of the rarest. **See page 29**

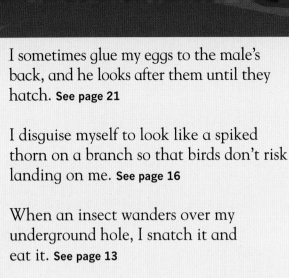

Gold beetle

Assassin bug

Katydid

Grasshopper

Indian moon moth

Trapdoor spider

Hawker dragonfly

Worker bee

Queen Alexandra's birdwing

Puss moth caterpillar

First flight

START

The caterpillar is on its way to becoming a butterfly. Follow it on its journey through the park and be the first one to see it transform into a butterfly!

Run into a spider.
Move back 3

Get food from the ant colony.
Move forward 2

Hide from a big bird.
Move back 3

A wise old owl shows the way.
Move forward 5

A praying mantis is hiding in the leaves.
Wriggle back 2

Get a ride from a bee.
Move forward 4

How to play

This game is for up to four players.

You will need
A die
Counters—one for each player

Move down **Move up**

Trace over the butterfly outlines or cut and color your own from cardboard. Each player takes turns throwing the die and begins from the START box. Follow the squares with each roll of the die. If you land on an instruction, make sure you do as it says. Good luck!

Find a tasty leaf to chew.
Move forward 4

Get help from a ladybug family.
Throw again

Stop to chat with a snail.
Skip a turn

FINISH
Spread your wings and fly!

Turn into a pupa.
Skip a turn

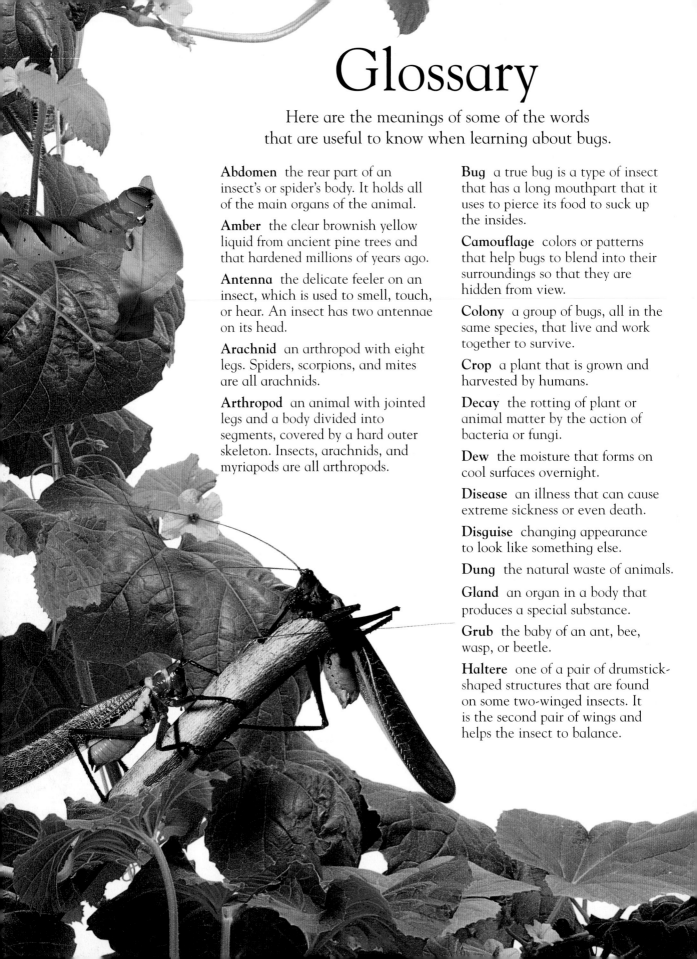

Glossary

Here are the meanings of some of the words
that are useful to know when learning about bugs.

Abdomen the rear part of an insect's or spider's body. It holds all of the main organs of the animal.

Amber the clear brownish yellow liquid from ancient pine trees and that hardened millions of years ago.

Antenna the delicate feeler on an insect, which is used to smell, touch, or hear. An insect has two antennae on its head.

Arachnid an arthropod with eight legs. Spiders, scorpions, and mites are all arachnids.

Arthropod an animal with jointed legs and a body divided into segments, covered by a hard outer skeleton. Insects, arachnids, and myriapods are all arthropods.

Bug a true bug is a type of insect that has a long mouthpart that it uses to pierce its food to suck up the insides.

Camouflage colors or patterns that help bugs to blend into their surroundings so that they are hidden from view.

Colony a group of bugs, all in the same species, that live and work together to survive.

Crop a plant that is grown and harvested by humans.

Decay the rotting of plant or animal matter by the action of bacteria or fungi.

Dew the moisture that forms on cool surfaces overnight.

Disease an illness that can cause extreme sickness or even death.

Disguise changing appearance to look like something else.

Dung the natural waste of animals.

Gland an organ in a body that produces a special substance.

Grub the baby of an ant, bee, wasp, or beetle.

Haltere one of a pair of drumstick-shaped structures that are found on some two-winged insects. It is the second pair of wings and helps the insect to balance.

Hive the home of honeybees.

Host the animal that provides a home for bugs, such as fleas or lice, that live off it.

Insect an arthropod with three body parts and six legs.

Larva the very young stage of an insect that looks completely different from its parents.

Metamorphosis the change from young to adult in an insect that looks completely different from its parents.

Migration moving from one place to another to live for a while, most commonly to find better weather.

Myriapod a type of arthropod with many legs, such as a centipede or millipede.

Nectar a sweet liquid found in many flowers.

Perfume a pleasant smelling liquid that attracts a type of animal to it.

Plague a group of insect that is out of control and causes trouble.

Pollination when tiny grains fertilize female plants to produce seeds and grow new plants.

Pollution dirty gases and waste from factories and cars that make the air, land, or water unclean.

Predator an animal that hunts other animals for food.

Prey an animal that is hunted by other animals as food.

Proboscis a tubelike mouthpart used by some insects to suck up liquid food.

Pupa the hard case in which some young insects completely change to become a different adult shape (during metamorphosis).

Recycle to treat materials in such a way that they can be used again.

Saliva the watery liquid, which is in the mouth, that helps to digest food.

Solitary being or living alone.

Swarm a mass of bugs, such as bees or locusts, that stick together to eat or find a new home.

Thorax the part of the body between the head and the abdomen on an insect. The legs and wings are attached to this part.

Vegetarian bugs that survive by eating just plants and no meat.

Venom a poison that is injected into another animal to paralyze or kill it.

Web a structure of fine silk threads spun by spiders and used to trap small bugs.

Wingspan the measurement from one wing tip to the other wing tip when they are fully open.

Index

Acknowledgments

Dorling Kindersley would like to thank:
Dorian Spencer Davies for original illustrations; and Sarah Mills for picture library services.

Picture credits:

The publisher would like to thank the following for their kind permission to reproduce their photographs:
a=above; c=center; b=below; l=left; r=right; t=top; f=far

BBC Natural History Unit: Bruce Davidson 42cla; Premaphotos 27bl. **Densey Clyne Productions:** Densey Clyne 55br. **Bruce Coleman Ltd:** Jane Burton 14cra; Andrew Purcell 32bc; Kim Taylor 35bl. **Corbis:** Anthony Bannister/Gallo Images 44bl. **Dorling Kindersley:** Ted Benton 51clb, Natural History Museum, London 47c, 49cb, 51bl. **Dreamstime.**

com: Andrey Burmakin 50fcrb, Cammeraydave 53cr, Harry Lines 53br, Trahcus 47br. **Michael & Patricia Fogden:** 20tl; Michael Freeman 44cr; Dan Guravich 3. Michael & Patricia Fogden: 16ca; 31tl. **Frank Greenaway:** 29tl. **N.H.P.A.:** Anthony Bannister 31tr, 38cla; 37bc; G I Bernard 20-21; Mark Bowler 17ca; Stephen Dalton 6cra, 6-7, 8clb, 8crb, 8-9, 13cra, 35tr, 35cla; Daniel Heuclin 40cl; Stephen Krasemann 18tr; Haroldo Palo Jnr 38tr; Peter Pickford 26; Dr Ivan Polunin 36-37. **Natural History Museum:** 22-23, 56cra. **Oxford Scientific Films:** Katie Atkinson 27tl; G I Bernard 33bl; Jack Clark 5, 45c; Fabio Colombini 2; S A L Cooke 41tr; Satoshi Kuribayashi 18cla, 24tl; London Scientific Films 23; Mantis Wildlife Films 37tr; L Martinez 13tr; Paulo de Oliveira 7tl; Tim Shepherd 15. **Papilio Photographic:** Robert Pickett 22cla. **Premaphotos Wildlife:** Ken Preston-Mafham 17tr, 19, 38tl. **Science Photo Library:** Darwin Dale 37tl, 41cla; Eye of Science 34; Dr Morley Read 39; Nuridsany & Marie Perennou 44cl; David M Schleser/Nature's Images 16-17; Jean-Philippe Varin/Jacana 30tl; Kazuyoshi Nomachi 40-41; Art Wolfe 17tl; Paul Zahl 13bl. **Telegraph Colour Library:** Hans Christian Heap 28cla. **Woodfall Wild Images:** Andy Harmer 13cla; Peter Wilson 14tl; David Woodfall 8-9. **Jerry Young:** 4c.

All other images © Dorling Kindersley
For further information see: www.dkimages.com